celtic cross
COLORING DESIGNS
VOL 1

A book of Celtic Cross coloring designs for calmness and relaxation

PUBLISHED BY
MoonSwept Press
20203 Goshen Road #374
Gaithersburg, MD 20879
©2018. All Rights Reserved
ISBN: 9781600870095

Get more coloring books, planners, and journals at
LifeLoveBizPrintables.com

www.ingramcontent.com/pod-product-compliance
Lightning Source LLC
Chambersburg PA
CBHW080943040426
42444CB00015B/3435